In his essay, "The Superiority of the Natural Image in Poetry," Arlice W. Davenport says, "the natural image can carry a poem, supplying its metaphors, its ideation, its resonant emotions." His latest book from Meadowlark Poetry Press, *Kind of Blue*, convinces the reader with delightful evidence of his thesis; witness these lines: ". . . cottonwoods / that carry their mortal burden / on their heads . . . speak / only in sign language / mincing words / a human could not say" ("Crossing the Field"). Jazz buffs will take note that this book shares the title of trumpeter Miles Davis' groundbreaking 1959 album, which added—to jazz musicians' traditional repertoire of improvisation based on chord progressions—the freedom of roaming the varied scales of modal jazz. Davenport's *Kind of Blue* appears like a burgeoning rebirth of natural imagery, conveying what he has to say in his own unique and refreshing idiom. He harnesses here the matched brace of *Metaphor and Mysticism: two things are the same, or one thing becomes another* (in "Zabriskie Point," he tells of the "broken mirror of touch:" in "The Return," ". . . the enigma of arrival the enigma / of being there . . ."). Similarly brilliant examples of metaphor ("Mountains tonsure clouds like ancient poets / skirting ponds" ("Fire on Fire"), "I juggle sounds like old skins of wine" ("Silence"), "I wear the weather like a cloak. / It wraps around my knees, massages my neck." ("Black")) and mystery ("I harbor strands of images in sources, sources / in substance, substance in images ad infinitum" ("Silence"), "Literature strains toward a flourish / of smoke. Not even the poet inhales." ("Smoke")) abound in *Kind of Blue*.

True to the title, the color blue provides a coherent and binding framework, a latitude and longitude for skyscape and seascape ornamented with imagery in varied modes, varied scale degrees of blue. Davenport quotes Wassily Kandkinsky, "Almost without exception, blue refers to the domain of abstraction and immateriality," then counters with "Bluebells, blueberries, blue wings on the jay, / Who says this is not nature's true color?" ("Blue"). As a scientist, I know that blue is indeed rare in nature, occurring most often as light refracted into blue wavelengths by structural scattering, but Davenport seems to find the color everywhere: "deep cyan, dark as night," "Indigo streets," "placid azure," "Aquamarine brings green to bear on the equation," "smoky blue valley," "Sea reflects sky reflects sea reflects a kind of blue." Here is blue so deep it becomes black: "Shadows don black overcoats, fedoras and masks," and even the brightest warm colors are complements of blue: "Jewels simmer in flames of orange," ". . . the ragged / window screens / letting in butterflies patchworks / of orange and blue."

Arlice W. Davenport has written two previous powerful and lovely books of poetry. *Kind of Blue* is a departure, built upon that foundation, an obvious coalescence (an encompassing?) of the strength, beauty, intelligence, and vigor of his prior work that becomes an appreciation of a life well-lived, well-traveled, well-shared, and now also well-considered, almost a *vade mecum* in verse for a life's experiences: "Poetry is a trail only prophets can walk" ("At Play in the Fields of Existenz"), "Poetry is no match / for death. Still, I write as though eternity descends in time" ("Silence"), ". . . all creatures on the odyssey home / carrying the blue jewels of the day / on their heads and backs. . ." ("Homecoming"). *Kind of Blue* is a book of exuberance, but one that does not take shortcuts, one whose emotions run in deeper currents, one that does not shy from philosophy, from art, from introspection: ". . . they say home is but a mirage the voyage forward / shimmers as the only place of belonging / may I still have eyes turned inward when I reach it" ("Icarus and Orpheus"). *Kind of Blue* is a book I found myself at home in; I suspect you may find yourself a place here as well.

—Roy J. Beckemeyer, *Mouth Brimming Over*

Arlice W. Davenport's new collection of poetry, *Kind of Blue*, explores his past and present emotions, and contemplates his place in the universe. He invites the reader to transcend the realm of the everyday and mundane, and challenges each one to become "illuminated" with him.

Through his intelligent verse, Davenport walks the tightrope between life and death, tangible and intangible, concrete and ephemeral. He draws his inspiration from celestial bodies, *objets d'art*, and later through nature. The cloudy landscapes of Cumbria become the playground of this poet and philosopher. Take a walk through these fields with him and become transformed by his words.

—**Elegia, founder of the Indelible Poetry Club on** *All Poetry*, **the world's largest poetry website**

Arlice W. Davenport's *Kind of Blue* is emotionally affluent, a broad-spectrum work that showcases his ability to make words live as transformative waves lapping our souls. His ideas inspire us to breach the mundane and enter realms of possibility, change, and spiritual ascension.

Davenport is an unashamed intellectual, giving his poems a philosophical scope that weaves imagery and thought together, leading us into worlds unknown.

Above all, this work will touch your heart quietly and fruitfully. Whether he is exploring the echoes of history or the allure of mysticism, Davenport's detailed touch ensures that each poem in *Kind of Blue* will continue to resonate upon re-reading, vibrant and profound.

—**Tony DeLorger, poet and author**

KIND OF BLUE

KIND OF BLUE

New Poems by **Arlice W. Davenport**

arlice w. davenport
Poetry can cure your
blues.

Meadowlark
PRESS
Emporia, Kansas, USA

Meadowlark Press, LLC
meadowlarkpoetrypress.com
P.O. Box 333, Emporia, KS 66801

Kind of Blue

Cover art by Norman Carr, *Midnight Melody,* acrylic on canvas

Author photo by a fellow traveler in Spain

Cover design by Norman Carr

Interior design by Linzi Garcia

POETRY / General
POETRY / Subjects & Themes / Inspirational & Religious
POETRY / Subjects & Themes / Nature

ISBN: 978-1-956578-18-8
Library of Congress Control Number: 2022941508

For Laura

Wandering the golden sands
of North Beach, you beam, my beacon
of hope, of life. Like a lighthouse
perched near a rocky shore, you encircle me,
illuminating our love
and the ever-elusive paths to safety.

Preface

In this new collection of poems, what I hope to achieve is a more immediate, Zen-like effect of illumination for the reader. Relying on motifs that reveal the presence of Being shining through my poems, I employ two major literary devices to achieve the desired state: metaphor as "this is that" and mysticism as "like becomes like."

Why do this? I think a case can be made that both devices aim at the same goal: unity of identity. Metaphor doesn't say that "this is like that;" there, we are in the territory of simile. Rather, metaphor identifies/unites two disparate objects (of thought or feeling or nature). They are distinct, but *each is the same*, to allude to Garcia Lorca. Likewise, the mystic's "like becomes like" indicates a process of unity, oneness, and intertwining essences.

I would love for readers to come away from this book feeling drawn to a type of mysticism that can nurture them and change their vision of the world. Rilke wrote in "Archaic Torso of Apollo," *You must change your life.* If my poems can even creep near that type of profundity, I would be satisfied.

One stylistic note: Many of the newer poems—especially those in the New Blue section of this book—have no to little punctuation. This is in homage to the late poetic style of W. S. Merwin, my favorite American poet. If it was good enough for him . . .

Also by Arlice W. Davenport

POETRY
Setting the Waves on Fire (Meadowlark P, 2020)
Everlasting: Poems (Meadowlark Poetry P, 2021)

Table of Contents

SEA BLUE

NEW BLUE

POSTLUDE

PRELUDE

*"Almost without exception,
blue refers to the domain of
abstraction and immateriality."*
–Wassily Kandinsky

Ancient Seers on the Wind

We spring up from shadows
into rocky gray fields
great stones sliced in half
by blades of wind
outcroppings cradle creatures
unable to thrive
they carry homes in their heads
nothing tangible or real
we too dwell among ideas that echo
through woods anemic cries
of vulnerability and loss
we clamor for a clear path forward
past dens of despair that hold captive
minds unwilling to be the self
they must become like weeds
they sprout in unlikely places
sucking up nutrients and light
transforming shadows into white
watching gray fields of rock
yield meadows dappled in wildflowers
the way ahead made clear
by ancient seers on the wind

Blue

The blue of a glacial lake lures the hiker to its shores.
He shivers from the water's icy touch.

Reflected on the mirrored surface,
blue mountains rise to the sky.

Sky, too, is blue, a paler version,
burned daily by the sun.

Blue impasto cakes the canvases of van Gogh.
He marries blue to yellow on his sacred color wheel.

Wallace Stevens wrote "The Man With the Blue Guitar."
It is a modernist classic. Yet who reads the poem today?

Joni Mitchell sings "Blue"—*Songs are like tattoos /
You know I've been to sea before.* Your spine shivers.

Bluebells, blueberries, blue wings on the jay.
Who says this is not nature's true color?

The dead turn blue before they creak into rigor mortis.
Blue eyes shed tears at the loss of the living.

Blue sapphires glitter in the blue-blood world of high
    fashion.
Blue blooms the hue of life. No one blinks twice.

SKY BLUE

"Cobalt is a divine color, and there is nothing so beautiful for creating atmosphere."

–Vincent van Gogh

Desire

We gather in circles
around the sacred stone,
waiting until the sky renews
the hour of our longing,
waiting until the stone speaks,
then caresses the fields
with blooms of lavender and rose.

The sun disperses clouds,
edges toward the firmament.
Through a tear in the cobalt dome,
I splatter white paint against it.
Stars sprout from my drippings,
soaring ever higher to new perches.
The brush flings of its own accord.

White spots transmute
into interlocking galaxies,
milky and pink, streaked
with flames of orange. Touching
the boundaries of the self,
constellations urge us upward.

We can escape mortality only
if we recite the everlasting word,
spoken on the wind. It heals
and renews, revives and succors,
gives hope to the desolate,
dispenses wisdom and the will
to enact it as spiritual discipline.

The word reshapes our destiny
as the poetics of the blind,
forever silent, save for what is spoken:
transcendent, everlasting, forged

in the fire of our primal yearning,
our anguished desire
that echoes off facets of the sacred stone,
which casts its heavy shadow
across layers upon layers.

Fire on Fire

1.

Smoke buoys behind the limestone wall.
Ashes trail flames, marching single-file.
Somewhere, my misplaced blazer burns,
found object of the night. Navy gold.

Mountains tonsure clouds like ancient poets
skirting ponds, reciting Confucian teachings,
watery poems. How the Orient still smiles
on us. At dusk, Chinese verses soar. Swans glide.

2.

Plum wine dribbles down my chin. Chopsticks
stab at rice, scrape edges of bowls. To indulge
at supper dulls the calligrapher's quills, wrenches
the novice's gut. Fasting alone inspires.

I have invested my heritage in black scrawls on parchment.
A jagged road map of singed stumps and empty barns.
Harvest never comes. Clouds of smoke billow past
skittering horses. They whinny for air, pure and golden.

3.

Our love sets fire on fire, consuming fuel for flitting
flames. I scribble epic poems on your palm.
A clenched fist erases meaning; images tumble
to the ground. You trample the limestone trail.

Heat excites my muse; she jitters before forms
of beauty, Plato's dialogues in hand. The Greeks
saw gods as swans, painted folly on their faces, seared
lust from their loins. Prometheus steals fire for mystic poets.

At Play in the Fields of Existenz

1.

Shadows don black overcoats, fedoras
and masks. They travel under
the noonday sun. Trailing them through
time: a bright undercurrent of gold.

I have embraced the V-ing branches
of oaks as they rise to scrape the sky. I have
exchanged stanzas with the whispering winds,
who chant only the glory of change.

England witches water to fill the brilliant lakes
that Coleridge and Wordsworth sang. I circle
Rydall Water in a typical nor'western downpour.
Even stale, lichen-stained caves offer no relief.

2.

Poetry is a trail that only prophets can walk.
Visionaries sketch out revelations on black slate
boards chained to schoolhouse desks. Wordsworth
carved his name into one, a pair of crooked W's.

My overcoat is black, my fedora and mask, too.
I join the single file of shadows. They shuffle
toward Ambleside and splash blue tides on lake beds.
I could write a glorious poem, but then I would be known
outside the circle of black, alone on the fells,
searching for water to wash myself clean.

Deep and Diffuse

Light filters through the bedroom window,
casting a cross between us on the rumpled sheet.

We commune with the dawn, beginning anew,
thrown into the world, wondering and opaque.

Jewels simmer in flames of orange and red.
Rays prism into the endless geometry of white.

Colors shimmer between the lines of our love, sketch
portraits of ourselves lying in wait, fevered and swift.

On the table, oranges anticipate their morning departure,
fragrant rinds, hemispheres of red-gold, succulent delight.

A ring of coffee stains the table, battered, scarred
from decades of use. The sheen of elbows: everlasting.

I watch you saunter into the world, needing *nada*.
How might underwrites your beauty, goodness and mind.

Light dwells in the habitation of the heart, deep, diffuse.
It erases all doubts of identity: son, daughter of the day.

Silence

1.

From silence, we return to silence.
Out of language, we reinvent ourselves.
The Other hears our sounds turned
words turned signs turned sounds.
We speak only fire in the smoky village.

I scrawl spidery marks on blank parchment,
connect them to thoughts and things,
project meaning to sate my senses.
I harbor strands of images in sources, sources
in substance, substance in images *ad infinitum*.

2.

A goldfinch balances at the feeder,
silently dancing within. Feral cats prowl
the premises, salivating for a taste
of life of death of nature's violence,
the bloody law: tooth, muscle, claw.

In the distance, clouds gather in clumps of gray,
heralding the deluge in which we shall drown.
A saving ark remains buried in Genesis,
the way forward lodged in the burning sky.
O to march in silence, serene and secure.

3.

I juggle sounds like old skins of wine. They do not
balance in the wind: full, bottom-heavy. Hemingway
guzzled from them on a bus through Spain, headed
for big-hearted fishing, a matter of life and death,
as was any task for the wounded surgeon of prose.

Driving an ambulance in the Great War, he died
inwardly. A black shadow, ragged at the edges,
followed him like a lost dog. Tail wags in silence,
lures him to a shotgun in Idaho. Poetry is no match
for death. Still, I write as though eternity descends in time.

Winds

At last, when the winds came,
the pottery lay broken upon
stone. Branches snapped
in syncopation. Waterfowl
scurried for cover. The sun dozed.

Your dress billowed like a robe
of minuscule shells, casting back
the glower of clouds. On the heel
of your hand, I read the calligraphy
of time. Veins pulsed, incognito.

Aphorisms of love spilled beneath
our feet. *Turn right, turn left, turn
inward toward the light,* only to sully
the forms of seeing, only to sigh for
respites from respiration. Lungs deflate.

The dog lunged toward us, laughing
at the lightness of being. The will wilts
into smoke, vapors spill into sky, sky
swirls into sand, sand fills hourglasses
like rain. In shadow, moments vanish.

Fires growl on the hills, scorched in acres
of sorrow. How the weak wither in the conqueror's
gaze. How fine the seeds of contemplation,
how vast the canvas of colors that bleed
to the edge of desire. Eyes shutter in gloom.

I mourn the loss of your reckless dance, snaking
into the crater. Embers shimmer like gems,
steam drenches strands of your hair, flames lick
the side of your face. Death delivers no clarity. Dreams
conjure grace. Winds lasso days. Pots reassemble.

Skunk Moon

Double moon buries stars.
Pitted spheres of pallid colors.
Caladium climbs, searches for sun.
Heart-shaped centers bleed.

Grinding wheel resists gale.
Pitted stone heavy as sin.
Skunk scurries past wooden fence,
scurries back, its mind not right.

Think of Lowell and "Skunk Hour."
No urban noise disturbs my peace.
No electric light supplants my fire.
Wayward buoys bounce in the inky sky.

Heat broils skin alive. Globe burns,
mindless. Solace in canyons, caves.
Clouds darken, bloated with rain.
Birthing pangs. Delivery at noon.

Hills hurl the sun to dawn. Shadows flee.
I wander fields of stone,
scuff boots, pray for peace.
Eastern blue. Ghost moon rises.

Black

Dry lightning sizzles the night.
Your umbrella fences toward
a foe's laminated heart.
Touché touches no one in the rain.

My books spread across the hardwood
floor. Downpours push through the open
window until clouds gather above my desk.
I throw my nth draft against the wall to watch

it stick. Adhesion fades, words slither down
the drain. Red edits correct themselves.
Revise, rewrite, rewind. With time, we practice
French verbs under the portico. Conjugations

copulate, clipped accent marks mate in the air.
We sip shadows, then sun in Provençal markets.
Antique fountain pens stir indigo ink, fat margins
diet until slim, slip into new robes. White is so passé,

but ushers in the new black. I wear the weather like a cloak.
It wraps around my knees, massages my neck.
O how the body knows it own, as we know ours.
Selves contain infinity, space-time, the Absolute, night.

Matter and spirit hunker down on the sideline: *stuck inside
of Mobile with the Memphis blues again.* We empty
cartridges of colors into the rusty well. Raise the bucket
to irrigate *les fleurs du mal.* Night, too, reeks of black.

Kind of Blue

1.

The promise of creativity
flows like rain pebbling
the roof of the study
where your untidy poems lie.
A glance backward
sweeps the world:
as rotund as an orange,
as blue as the books
we pack in refrigerated boxes.
A deep cyan, dark as night,
settles over the city. Indigo
streets, limned avenues.
Dreams encased in dreams.

2.

Waters wash over me,
a placid azure stitched
with maroon and gray. I marvel
at them in autumn on the streets
of Scotland, blood-red moon
ascending over Edinburgh's castle.
Black, black sky, the fingerprints
of God pressed onto burnt-out suns.
Novas, nuevas, née mort.
I would tally the containers,
but the abacus is broken.
All numbers equal nine.
Aquamarine brings green
to bear on the equation.

3.

Salt seeps through the hollows
of walls, the room interrogates
itself in pools of seaweed, soft-
shelled crabs, angular gulls.
You know the ocean's rhyme,
but the meter is skewed, the skewer
heavy with charbroiled fish.
No plates, forks. Sea reflects sky
reflects sea reflects a kind of blue,
exonerates my mood. Trumpet trills
shrink the shallow hue of veins. Blood
pumps blue pumps red pumps life
on the cathedral steps. O-negative breaks
positive. I will sweep up the pieces,
paint them steely blue.

Zabriskie Point

1.

The mind replenishes itself
in stark pirouettes of light.

Body kisses soul,
the inrush of blood,
tingling, desire.
The broken mirror of touch.

O how eternal union eludes us.
O how the night sweeps up
pieces of dawn,
scatters them
like stones
from a cairn toppled
in the wind.

2.

Fleurs de lis, fleurs du mal.
Hammer the symbol to clang
like a gong. Hammer the hearer
to echo like a gorge: *life, knife, strife.*
Immortality swoons
at the grave of a blue moon.

Ask for excess, more
than you could want.

Ask for redemption from
being-unto-death.
Throw yourself back
into the world.
Urge the Other

to shepherd what is.
Urge the Other
to shadow what is not.
Urge the Other
to care for the great mystery.

Smoke

Solar flares scorch
the galaxy.
Stars swirl
counterclockwise,
confused.

The world is white
on white,
orbiting the path
of Prometheus'
blanching fire.

I walk beneath
the night sky,
aimless as
ocean currents:
surging, surging, retreat.

Do stars guide us,
conscious of space
and time? They carry
no message or *telos*.
Stardust. Evergreen.

The poem rises
on its own.
I write it as
singeing dictation.
It burns my ear and eye.

I will weave garlands
of prairie grasses.
Rectangular plains
carry no star.

My voice withers, inflamed.
Literature strains toward a flourish
of smoke. Not even the poet inhales.

Shadows on the Wall

Fields disappear.
Darkness blankets the hills.
We laugh on a low, stone wall
extending to the void.
We face the moon: off-white
with an orange tinge
The sky is not our own.
We laugh again at the paucity
of thought.

The enormity of silence.
Desire disrupts all conventions.
Like archaeologists, we dig, dig, dig
deep into arid soil, uncovering
lost cities, mosaics, pottery still usable.
But no self. It leaves no traces.
Evanescent, invisible, it lurks
on the perforated edge of things.

An empty box, a casket.
Praise the dead for being
carried into the future.
Only bones rule now, pale runes.
We read them without a key.
We embrace contradictions.
We say yea and nay,
and they resound as one.

Savor ambiguities.
Throw oil on fire. Does it still burn,
or smoke profusely?
Heat escapes the night.
Cold bones assemble
in humanity's artifice. We recognize

Platonic forms of man, woman.
We dispel the shadows on the wall,
then rise to the glistening light.

Vision

Eyes twitch in the mounting breeze.
Storms build on the bruised horizon.

Clouds cluster above wavering trees,
dump lakes of rain on the dry arroyo.

I sense the barometer of floods encroach,
soon to submerge the Earth in roiling waves.

No dove speeds toward us, no olive branch blooms.
Only chaos persists in its darkened clutches.

Heed Nature's anger, indiscriminately thrown
at every living being sans innocence.

Arm yourself against the threatening signs:
Desolation is the plague that never ends.

The Crack in the Mirror

My voice lost deep
inside me, I silently
stare at the looking glass.
Staring back is the face
of Narcissus. I strain
to recognize the eyes,
a deep sky blue,
but know they are not mine.

My thoughts lost deep
within me, I meditate
on mystics who teach
that virtue can cheat death.
I struggle to discern
the immortality of my goodness,
but notice only the fevered crack
in the glass. It, too, is not mine.

My dreams, lodged far
beyond me, I call to them
to return to the surface
of my mind, as immortal
as the Good, as untouchable
as the mirror image. I close
my eyes to conjure them,
but the scenes are not mine.

My hopes, linked tight
beside me, glimmer
like raindrops in the sun.
I grasp at reflections
of tomorrow, curved pictographs
of what could come. I clinch
my fist to capture them,
but they glide away into the mist
that can never be mine.

Dawn's New Name

Fields of light flicker as night descends.
The Encompassing fills black holes,
doles out excess riches across the leaden sky.

Trees lower their arms in quiet rest.
Skeletal fingers scratch out calligraphy:
a palindrome, dawn's new name.

A traveler raises the shade on his room's
unpainted window, unfurls shutters,
imbibes the drunken fragrance of rain.

Brushstroke shadows spread along
the wall. He splashes his face, towels away
a residue of soap, his visage renewed

in a portraiture of hope. How he yearns
for a cup of freshly brewed coffee, for the taste
of promise on his chipped, white plate.

Light births the day, a hairline crack in a mirror.
Black becomes the new white. The Encompassing
dons a robe, stitches in dawn's new name: *Eve.*

Arias

As it always has been
soundless dreams
populate the night sky
translucent globes
rattle with tumbling
imagery and confused
movements of the mind
shuttered visions
defuse the moods
of passion and fear
anger and sorrow
I sift them in hushed
tones a spectrum
of unknown choices
of unheard arias

"Oh soft kisses, oh sweet abandon,
As I trembling
Unloosed her veils and disclosed her beauty.
Oh vanished forever is that dream of love,
Fled is that hour,
And desperately I die.
And never before have I loved so much!"

O how can we return
from the death
of dreams how feed
on the word
only to starve
as time
is devoured by rust
we carry the blight
within us as we
pass through
the narrow gate

iron has painted
the stones
a rusty brown
with orange added
at the edges
how many unseen
flaws lie hidden
in the emptiness within
in the way
of shadowed sight
how much love
is lost

"The love that found the way to save your life
Shall be our guide on earth, our pilot on the waters,
And make the wide world lovely to our eyes;
Until together we shall fade away
Beyond the sphere of earth, as light clouds fade,
At sundown, high above the sea."

The quotations are from Giacomo Puccini's opera Tosca.

Winter's Tale

When it is time
to bring in the sunken
summer sun
the barn will
light up like
a satellite barreling
through space
a bright star shielded
from the void
as it will be until
there is no more light

Winter buries life
in a casket of ice
lying atop the hard
frozen soil
forlorn as a deer
cut off from
its herd
when I climb
the fields
of untrammeled snow
geese honk at my
trespassing
as I forgive
their trespasses
against me
if winter were my home
I would forever flee

Richard Strauss'
Don Juan symphony
surges on the airwaves
a paean to lust to life
to the fatal lure

of love that snares
the unwitting seducer
who will hibernate
with the sun
no heat no light
no sustenance
in the frigid dark

I will open wide
the barn door
and let the rays
of renewal
spread across
the blackness
of winter's shroud
which weighs
so heavily
upon my shoulders

The Return

What returns is never the same
smelling of afternoon sun
clothed in dust motes
that clutter the room
sheet music on the piano yellows
to leave is to forsake
the innuendo and rumor
of the social self squeezed
into bourgeois aspirations
of material comfort and success
endless power over the Other
they must be burned to begin again

Out of the cluster of oaks
I clamber across the grasslands
they sway as diverse in their strength
as the berries that weigh down the ivy
brushing against the face of my home
I do not judge them they ignore me
their perfect spheres taunting my need
for order beauty the seasons turning
and so I am back hunting them
gathering them washing them in cold water
tasting their outer layer of flesh then the hint
of sweetness waiting in their darkened core

All discoveries are new mysterious
seedily mundane they compose
the enigma of arrival the enigma
of being-there to wrestle eternity and time
to outrun death lodged in our chests
like a riddled heart pumping poison
that spills out of capillaries and veins
soaks into our socks bathes our knees
splashes into the bowels of life which circle

monotonously on the weaver's spindle
fabric embryonic in its strands
is about to appear textured colored marked
in dyes the ancestors raised from the earth

I would not remain but the owl cries stir in me
the lust to fly after prey to swoop down
on the unsuspecting jewel hidden
in clumps of earth overturned
by the plow I will write a new self
on the wing wedded to the hills
rich in simple things finding my way
through the milky shadows of deepest night
the muffled calls of the return

BEFORE BLUE

"Where did you get your eyes so blue?
Out of the sky as I came through."
–George MacDonald

Heavy as Stone

1.

Footholds on the wall fill in
like skittish gull prints at low tide.
All form vanishes into liquid,
all liquid cements into form.

I have climbed over stones larger
than the world. I have cradled egos
in crooks of trees. I have brushed against
the void before crumbling into dust.

Fluorescent meadows feed throngs
of cattle and sheep. Bells punctuate
the air with an abstract melody.
Soon birds will echo it as they mate.

2.

I have built altars unknown to the wind.
I have recorded voices of angels in my sleep:
*Fear not. Abandon yourself to the road
still taken. Cultivate simplicity. Harvest joy.*

The wall divides this life from the next.
Its footholds have vanished. Waters wash
over the surface like mountain streams.
I catapult into the future, boxing solid air.

Starlings flutter, lie dead on the road.
The sky will not buoy them, the earth
claims its own. There is no joy on the mountain,
only simplicity. I carry it away, heavy as stone.

Big Two-Hearted River

Hand the horizon sandy hillocks
that hide the heaving sea.
Breathe in the effervescent
spray of brine soaked
into the blustery breeze.
Fruits congregate like captives
of a hooded Inquisition.
Watch them sweat and blink.

Waves spray-paint the sand
in vanishing fringes of white.
I splash through what remains
of low tide, searching for *je ne sais quoi*.
Baptism protects from darkness within,
but the sea is no respecter of persons.
It sucks up shadows, spews them into
blacker depths: dog-paddle or drown.

Shells litter my path, small creatures
freed of form, ready to reinvent
themselves, but powerless to crawl
into the future. An orange peel perfumes
their bed, unmade in the open air.
Light dances on their new home, seeping
from within, a nascent exoskeleton,
impotent shield from despair.

Clouds, plump with rain, collide midair;
their underbellies link in conspiracy
against the land. My pilgrimage
advances uneasily, the map long thrown aside,
the X turned Z, smeared by clumsy thumbs.
I cut rough bread, pungent cheese, a half-bottle of red wine
in my pack. The big two-hearted river irrigates
my mind. Hidden hillocks hold back the sea.

SEA BLUE

"Roll on, thou deep and dark blue ocean."
–Lord Byron

The Kingfisher

"As kingfishers catch fire, dragonflies draw flame . . ."
—**Gerard Manley Hopkins**

Here in the great marsh of solitude
where each step sucks up a sludge
of mud and withering reeds, I search
for the kingfisher, who spears his prey
with the speed of light, swallows it
whole, then clown-walks through
waves that lap his anorexic knees.

Hopkins sets the bird on fire, iridescently
burning through his unmanacled poem.
Immanence and transcendence meld
like bronze and steel. Creation: one glorious
feat, one marvelous miracle splashing apart,
beyond our imagination. With the kingfisher,
we cry, *What I do is me: for that I came.*

I have slogged my way through muck,
undeterred by slow progress, undefeated
by the path alone, the path without end,
the path of unrequited promise. No companion
darkens my way, no mind nurtures my own.
Trailing the kingfisher, I trudge and slosh.
Selves—goes itself; myself it speaks and spells.

Sailing to Byzantium

1.

I shall no longer sail to Byzantium
with the ghosts of Lowell and Yeats.
The art: two-dimensional, too flat,
icons crashing gates of heaven,
snatching radiance and grace,
the grammar of delight.

Poetry will not redeem or save,
but preserves the *agons* of the age.
We wrestle with ourselves,
twin nemeses in flight, upright
in conflict, defeated when sight
no longer finds solace in the night.

2.

Waiting in the rain, steam rises
past buildings and streets,
past movements so fleet we count
them new in their ageless force.
Step lightly over swells
of urban tides, crabs ride

them to concrete shores
shot through with grime,
awaiting some crime to sling
new blood. No Byzantine
could depict this plight without
volume and weight, filigrees of light.

3.

Lowell's mind was not right.
Yeats chased spirits without fright.
The dead shared secrets he need not dread.
Life pushes on like a tendril in the sun,
stretching toward the endless One.
Darkness shatters in mid-write.

East of Eden

1.

How the bridge spans
currents of eternity.
How time crests the waves
of lowly human pain.
Silence, obedience chisel
into worlds of devotion.

Turn toward the flaming sword
that casts Adam east of Eden.
Turn toward the forbidden fruit
that lies rotting on the ground.
Evil has no home until
our will lodges it in history.

We choose solely in passionate
ignorance. We seek nothing
but the dreamlike good. Impulse
makes real what would otherwise
not happen: the insidious sovereignty
of sin. Blackened spoils of freedom.

2.

Now trodding the muck of trails
in nakedness, now without shame,
fully present in the garden, fully
creature before God. Who can dwell
in joy without the coil of hubris?
We slither along these paths ever alert

to the mortal Other, who speaks
loss of innocence, who spins
spells of cupidity. Each reflection

beams the face of Cain. Each
decision robs us of nature's
sanctity, the bounty of Being,

spread before us like a great banquet.
The marriage supper of the Lamb.
Grant servants freedom,
masters deep chests of coal.
All things fill the nothingness
of self. Few make the world habitable.

3.

Stellar ships sail under the bridge,
cast shadows far from the muddled shore.
Dark streams carry the pain of desire
beyond the confines of love.
Ecstatic foam breaks on the bank.
Empty canoes float idly by.

What passes for strength is but
algae feeding. Hand-hewn wells.
Living water cleanses into new life.
Adam abandons the old, trapped
in the *élan vital*, his vale of pain. We
do well to heed the moans, his sermon

of errancy and doubt. Purple berries
trampled underground, seeds buried in soil.
Trees flourish without Adamic names.
Birds serenade in clear, high notes.
Life moves of its own accord, pressing
ever outward, past Eden's eastern gate.

We Lose Ourselves

Emptiness fills each porous thing. Lightness,
wonder, astonishment. Forests, rivers
change their course. We practice
mindfulness as hawks kill sparrows.
Beak and talons. Bloodless cuts. Authenticity
dissolves in soups of clichés. Mystic
vision. Ecstatic union, boundless light.

In medias res, life interrupted.
A cruel light glimmers on the sea,
configured as desire. No one declares,
*You are, neck-deep in Being, armored
against the void.* Potent silences. Stones
stacked against tides. Crabs sidewind on sand.
Shadow of the Other's face. Alienation.

We reflect half-truths as we dip into shallows.
Rafts of words. Labyrinths of sighs.
We seek only sky, light of memory, lure
of sorrow. Inattention abounds. Gardens
bloom with joy. Koans replicate like mutant cells.
Severed blisters. Transfiguration. Pity impales,
close and warm. The unruly unite, recalculate.

Worlds filter flames. Heat moistens brows. Present
future past present. Weight of the moon flattens the mind.
Tapestries of wisdom unravel in flight. Vertiginous
heights, dark rooms at night. Presence hardens like steel.
Forgiveness shapes nothingness into breath. All things
illuminate, rejuvenate. We lose ourselves in poems.
Queen Anne chairs crowd the floor. Thrones of the dead.

No Map Needed

The architecture of my mind
catapults the past
into suspended animation,
hovering over barren lakes
like a hot-air balloon,
all jets firing, casting past
the crest of creation.

Still thriving
at the Omega point—
the end prophesied
in the beginning—
no one notices
the clumsiness
of dancing on air.

Fabric-encased
cubicles craft
the perfect black hole
of loneliness.
No light enters,
exits. Outside,
butterfly bushes
bloom in a lavender
cul de sac.
Keep right, keep right
to circle back.

Each uneven line
of the poem:
an epitaph for the living.
Mother Nature
throws out the bathwater,
plants the baby
on the throne. Long live

the king/queen/knave
of our golden
fiefdom.
       Serfs
follow seagull
tracks in the sand,
reach for an elixir
to cure
the queasiness
of sautéed crabs.

Guitars wail
the haunting
riffs of
"All Along
the Watchtower"
as we sail
'round the Cape
of Good Hope
hugging our African
roots. No map
needed, our clan
ensconced
in the savanna.

Faces on the waves.
Dreams long forgotten.
The past belly-flops
into the future.
Hot-air balloon
flattens as it lands.
Jets fire into grass, *finito*.
Who will sail again?

Domain

Outside the domain, we die marching—
a reluctant return to the tyrant's regime.
Tempted by the inhuman, we depart blind,
still shaken by the enormity of our loss.

Body and soul meld into one, trapped in glistening
webs of symbiosis. Yet body also rises as world.
The Age of Great Navigators has begun. Sails snap,
monoculars lunge, sailors tumble out of crow's nests.

They cling to rigging in midair. For the captain,
creativity and discovery bode the same. Land
pops up *ex nihilo*. A secret dimension decrees
our course. To follow it with abandon means

risking freedoms. But shuttered in darkness,
we decide, with no shame. River rocks mark
the path home. I kick them behind me, peering
through shadows at the perishing domain.

Nothing Else Pertains

1.

A pool of sorrow
washes over my feet.
I walk on waves
to avoid its depths.
From there, I shall float
to a cove of freedom.
It demands my all. It crawls
across my face like a marauding
mosquito. My blood flows
through the insidious syringe,
feeds the world's worst
sinners: parasites of the living,
slurping corpuscles like wine.

2.

The poem rises from nothingness
into Being, miracle of creation
bestowed on paltry yearnings.
Faithful steed through the long,
laborious night, the horse rears
against its rider. No one listens
to my lyric save the corpulent corpse
awaiting resurrection. I drink
the dregs of wisdom as they
spill my way. Do they cohere?
Does the wolf stalk the deer
through mystic forests?
Meaning no longer elicits
memory or will. Let it flow
through my mortal center, the still,
small voice of art. Watercolors
fade at the fringe of patterned paper.

Oil mixes with water, their hues
repeal the blanched face of death.

3.

Let us laugh at our weakness, painting gray
and wan the grand overtures to tragedy.
Fortunes fall and rise on tides of the banal.
This, the world haunted by God, swirling
with delusions of sovereignty,
with the impotence of choice.
Ride to the city gates. Let enemies fire
cannons, strike bells, burn books
of verse, enslave the soul
of the poet, who navigates homeward
through a tyrannical dark wood.

4.

Where Paradise begins, Inferno ends.
We climb the slippery slope of Purgatory,
striving to rise, rise, rise past the clutches
of sin. Once we arrive, we are lost
in the psychedelia of the beatific vision.
Behold, behold. Joy twists eternity
into a lock with key. Turn it tightly,
hear tumblers click, feel resistance,
never force. The gate gapes
at an embarrassment of riches:
la dolce vita. Eye gold dust
sloshing in the pan's crevices.
Eye the sold sign on St. Teresa's
interior castle. We are not made
for death, even as the maker's
mark fades in the sun, sinks
into the cove. Let us wash it clean
of error and lust. Here, nothing else pertains.

Twilight

"There is, then, a world immune from change. But I am not composed enough, standing on tiptoe on the verge of fire, still scorched by the hot breath, afraid of the door opening and the leap of the tiger, to make even one sentence. What I say is perpetually contradicted."
—**Virginia Woolf**

I ride the waves, weighed down
by the oceanic flux
that infiltrates our being.
Pitched headlong onto shore,
I am burned by sand,
tangled by seaweed, caught
in the mad grip of red-rock crabs
who scurry sideways around
my waterlogged body.

I peer over the blackened
wall of the other world.
What I see should
harrow me, but I look
with a voyeur's eyes,
caressing the void
of all I desire,
of all I have left behind,
of all that yet awaits.

The sea saturates my skin
with a sticky brine that
never runs dry. It stings
my eyes, shrivels every piece
of naked flesh. The sea
pummels the shore,
offers no excuse
for punishing
the lone swimmer.

At twilight, crabs burrow
in the sand like living stones.
The tide washes over them,
flicking every fleck of detritus
from their perilously soft shells.
Their armor needs an overhaul,
their gait must be straightened.
I toss a seashell at their heads,
dinging their flat faces, dotting

an eye with the mark of Cain:
suffering at the Other's whim
till death do them part. How
little love matters, contradicted
by the flesh, constrained
by chance, unable to utter
one true sentence,
one affirmation of the fire
that does not consume.

At dusk, tans turn blue turn
purple turn green. Grass grows
between grains of sand, planted
to infinity. I share my vision
with William Blake, the seer of heaven
and hell, of the tiger and the lamb,
of industry and the manacled soul.
That way lies the constancy of change,
the final triumph of the waves.

Big Sur

A hand-breaking chill. A cup of steaming coffee, its silver
breath lassos the sun, tightens its grip on red-black
flares that quickly spew warmth on the crooked coast
of Big Sur. Impatient with the 20-degree dawn, you gesture
to hit Highway 1 again, snaking northward to Paradise.

At the ocean, you dared me to rebuild Jeffers' stone tower,
its sights fixed on the sweeping purple-pink clouds that
     swayed
like clumps of prairie grasses. When I pass through those
     grasses,
I listen to hawks recite my pledge: To precision-cut each
     stone,
tattooing it with your timeless name, Original Friend.

*Robinson Jeffers, one of the great American modernist poets, built
a stone tower by hand known as Tor House, near Carmel-by-the-
Sea, California.*

To Some Far Water's Edge

I have traveled all directions
to arrive at the edge of your village
its battlements rising in black slate
its orange roofs clustered like a tiled choir
above the smoky blue valley
an attic chorus that chants
my every wayward step
as I descend the green mountain path
to the house that holds the emblem
of our union locked fast in its keep

When I walk toward you now it is always light
the fields arrayed in wildflowers purple
yellow red they thrive for a moment only
to wither and fade and return always return
with the errant wind at my back and I realize
I have not gained as much ground as before I left
next to the pitted stone wall I climb
the ridge and survey the western horizon
where we once joined bodies and minds
one intent one will one way forward

This valley bleeds into the river that curls
like a sea monster out of the ancient deep
what lurks beneath the surface rears up
and rockets through the waves to devour
all in its path here the river's bend cradles
the fringe of the forest that shrouds my way
I move beyond the ancestors' camp making
an inheritance for the life that springs up
through the fire of our touch I turn into the wind
bearing the ashes of the past to some far water's edge

The Dun-Colored Hills

Light breaks across
the aching brow
of the lonely hunter
hawks swoop around his head
he bows in reverence before
their skills navigating the skies
in search of cleanly plucked
feasts from the winnowing fields

I am no hunter I tramp
the roads beside the fields
one foot down then the other
a solitary parade led by songbirds
aroused from their slumber
by passing winds from unseen heights
I hear their cadence in the night

And think of Hemingway's big two-hearted river
carrying the woes of war downstream
in the wake of fishing a triumph over nature
a feast to soothe the tired brow
a prey that sheds no blood
but cleanses in streams of cold water
as light breaks across the dun-colored hills

The Dolphin

1.

The salon, slatternly and dim,
smells vaguely of opium.
Poems mingle in clouds, poets
recline around cups of wine,
à la Socrates in Plato's *Symposium.*

Baudelaire stands nearby, a devotee of art,
a slave to flawless beauty. He frightens me,
with a copy of *Madame Bovary* in hand,
a scimitar tucked in a greasy sash.
Cigar plumes pool below the frescoed ceiling.

2.

The dolphin dives into the shallowest depths,
backstrokes out to sea, swallows minnows
like caviar. Part fact part fiction part plaintive fact,
the dolphin wounds without empathy or thought.
The humiliation of others: the finest act of power.

Lowell frightens me more than Baudelaire. Tyrant
of his bloated fiefdom, he sacrifices all life, all love
on the altar of verse. A beating heart raised to the sun,
misery proves immortal for the *poète maudit.* "To perceive
is to suffer," moans Aristotle, squinting with his one good eye.

3.

Once the senses kick-start their vagabond dance,
every pillar of light shines brighter. *More is more is more*
moans the avaricious will. *I want, I want, I want* echoes
the maddened king. Every downpour heals his crooked
    sonnets.
The flowers of evil bloom perennially, but last only a season.

Schools of dolphins spiral backward, awe tourists
crowding the pool. Do they eat their young, mate for life?
Is love more vivid in a confessional poem? Is the dichotomy
of the self? Lowell reigns over the psych ward in a threadbare
robe. He flings a copy of *The Dolphin* at all spooning serfs.

The recently published The Dolphin: Two Versions, 1972-1973
*(Macmillan) is an expanded edition of Lowell's Pulitzer Prize–winning
provocative poetry collection that crossed the line between art and life.*

The Birth of Venus

1.

an intimate light breaks across the yellow beach
our footprints meld with gulls' trident steps
curtains of foam splash into basalt blocks
trickling streams deflect crabs' jerky crawls

we cheer the birth of Venus on the half-shell
golden-red tresses caress her alabaster skin
winds blow like cherubim spewing spume
from Bernini's pools   Jupiter turns, laughs with joy

2.

undone by love's embrace I wander between
stone and sea   a virgin fire burns in Venus' eyes
   diaphanous robes billow beside her scalloped throne
trees soar on the undulant shore   cliffs clap from on high

shall I hallow this vision with sacred song   shall I scoop
up waves to bathe her immaculate frame   she
rises as the Italians' hardened truth   no one can claim
her as his own   her face makes even Aphrodite moan

3.

we besiege her defenses to no avail   all attempts
to woo drown in undertow   at Uffizi she beams
a goddess' smile   pastels wash over us like
stinging brine   our imaginations bloom wider
than mythic love   we incarnate archetypes
of fickle gods   we await our birth into
the crimson dawn   into the sea that roils within the blue sea
into the luminous strands of burgeoning sky

NEW BLUE

"There are connoisseurs of blue just as there are connoisseurs of wine."
–Sidonie Gabrielle Colette

The Superiority of the Natural Image in Poetry

I have been preaching for some time now that the natural image can carry a poem, supplying its metaphors, its ideation, its resonant emotions. The natural image is imperiled in contemporary poetry, which drips with the guile of urban alienation or strives to reduce diction to a monosyllabic drone that avoids hard questions of meaning and form. And even though these "schools" have their place in the history of poetry, they rarely leave the reader feeling fulfilled, spoken to, or completed by the poem.

The natural image can cure these woes. And it does so in three primordial ways. First, it recapitulates the sense of a paradise lost, of the Eden our Ur-parents were rudely forced to leave, exiled to some far country of pain and turmoil east of the original garden. Second, it nurtures the self by reinstating its creaturehood; we as humans exist in a natural nexus with much of the world. Although that nexus is in profound peril from our own hubris and desecration of the globe, the poet can still revive the fellow-feeling that we carry deep below the layers of our conscious minds, and which places us smack dab in the middle of Nature with a capital "N," and thus in the ecological niche where we can thrive and create, becoming our own nature, seeking unity, integrity and a missing wholeness that perhaps even the natural image cannot provide. (More on this later, after you catch your breath.) Finally, natural imagery spurs our sense of stewardship; it reawakens our responsibility to care for what is. We are called out of Eden to oversee and help direct (as much as is humanly possible) the course of nature toward a better *telos*, toward a better end of flourishing, reproducing, and spreading the boundaries of its kingdom to the

next generation's delight, and to its fulfillment as an
enormous fellow creature.

These are heady remedies that poetry may not be
wholly able to deliver, as I said. W. H. Auden said of
poetry that it "might be defined as the clear expression
of mixed feelings." But he also declared that "poetry
makes nothing happen." Certainly, poetry is not
classically useful; there is not much that you can do with
a poem besides read and savor it. But poetry can spark
an existential awakening of finding ourselves once again
in the grip of nature, feeding off its bounty, cleaning up
its messes, building better shelters, husbanding better
vineyards, and marveling at the explosion of flora and
fauna gracing our lands.

How useful all this may be is up to the reader to
decide. In fact, most meanings of a poem come from
the reader's participation in making them. But poetry
can inspire, and the natural image willingly carries
this burden; it can evoke the *mysterium tremendum* that
rattles our bones and flames the fever of creating, of
ek-stasis, of the ineluctable movement outside ourselves
into the greater, nurturing whole. Not convinced?

Give it a try.

Of course, what this little essay needs is an example.
And below is a sophisticated one from, in my mind,
the greatest English poet of the first world war, Edward
Thomas. In it, he uses the familiar natural image of
plowing a field to encompass young love, the losses of
the war, and the tentative movements toward a genuine
conversation with the plowman. This should inspire
and prod us all to try to write in a similar fashion.
Reading Thomas, the reader is naturally and spiritually
quickened. It's hard to ask for anything more from a
contemporary poem. Change the world? How about
change the reader, then move on?

As the Team's Head-Brass

As the team's head-brass flashed out on the turn
The lovers disappeared into the wood.
I sat among the boughs of the fallen elm
That strewed an angle of the fallow, and
Watched the plough narrowing a yellow square
Of charlock. Every time the horses turned
Instead of treading me down, the ploughman leaned
Upon the handles to say or ask a word,
About the weather, next about the war.
Scraping the share he faced towards the wood,
And screwed along the furrow till the brass flashed
Once more.   The blizzard felled the elm whose crest
I sat in, by a woodpecker's round hole,
The ploughman said. "When will they take it away?"
"When the war's over." So the talk began—
One minute and an interval of ten,
A minute more and the same interval.
"Have you been out?" "No." "And don't want
to, perhaps?"
"If I could only come back again, I should.
I could spare an arm. I shouldn't want to lose
A leg. If I should lose my head, why, so,
I should want nothing more. . . . Have many gone
From here?" "Yes." "Many lost?" "Yes, a good few.
Only two teams work on the farm this year.
One of my mates is dead. The second day
In France they killed him. It was back in March,
The very night of the blizzard, too. Now if
He had stayed here we should have moved the tree."
"And I should not have sat here. Everything
Would have been different. For it would have been
Another world." "Ay, and a better, though
If we could see all all might seem good." Then
The lovers came out of the wood again:

The horses started and for the last time
I watched the clods crumble and topple over
After the ploughshare and the stumbling team.
—**Edward Thomas**

Crossing the Field

The chill in the air haunts
the black stones washed clean
by the tepid river
it flows past cottonwoods
that carry their mortal burden
on their heads they speak
only in sign language
mincing words
a human could not say
the ice floes have melted
the rains stopped
little moisture but my belabored breath
crossing the field
pheasants take flight
field mice scurry
the chill means nothing
to those ensconced in the earth

I have left and returned
smelling of honey and smoke
aromas of belonging
but I cannot say where
I have eaten the bitter fruit
of not being there
I carry my mortal burden
on my back wet with winter's chill
fires line the woods
the pond glazes over

I look far afield
but must camp alone

Anvil

I remember the anvil
unrung for years
a monolith of iron
its silver sheen glistening
from the hammer's
glancing blows

I remember the ragged
window screens
letting in butterflies
patchworks
of orange and blue
they knew not
where they were
or why the house stood

And already it was time
to leave summer
season of sticky skies
and uncut grasses
season of woods
and waters
season of no seasons

And already it is time
to return in winter
season of icy rooms
and quilted nights
season of driving south
on two-lane roads
cutting through
blue mountains
I'll Fly Away
on the radio

The anvil rings out
from nowhere
and everywhere
unmuffled
by its sawdust bed
unruffled
by the rough-hewn loft
pitched high above me

A dusty sheen
pushes its way
into cobwebbed
shadows
my uncle's
work gloves
on the anvil
a disarray
of leather
dirt and tears

And already it is time
for mourning
broken hands
and unseen dreams
this season
of no seasons
about to depart

Orion

(After William Stafford)

The doe, long gone cold,
looked weirdly back at me,
her neck broken, her eye
frozen in a wall-eyed stare
from the pit of death.

Her tawny hide leeched gray
flecks of fur. She had bartered
her beauty for one last leap
across the old wire fence.
Yesterday the hunters came.

Startled on my way back
to the car, I saw her hind leg
strangled in the top wire
of fencing, some farmer's pledge
to stay a good neighbor.

My shadow loped ahead of me
in the glow of a sleepy-eyed sun.
I was thinking how the river would
wash away the blood from my hands.
I was thinking about Faust and his folly.

At the car, I looked back, the deer's eye
black as sin. Now, she would no longer
search the night sky for the pointed tip
of Orion's arrow. Now, she no longer shivered
in the winter winds. Behind me, two guns fired.

A Darkening Sky

The scent of freshly mown alfalfa
perfumes the purple night sky.
My grandfather's ranch: no lights,
no houses, no people or machines
within 20 miles. He liked it that way.

He rode his horses in the silent dawn.
Massive beasts, they accepted
his small frame. The stables smelled
of saddles and hay and newly planed
wood. Nothing escaped his touch.

He watched me ape his movements
atop a painted pony. Tiny in the saddle,
I tried to exert my will, right then left. No
signal reached my partner. The horse loped
around the corral, hoping for food or rest.

When he died, my grandfather left
a long legacy. His spirit populated
the vast, rolling prairie. His horses
sold to respectful townsfolk
in need of lively companions.

I never mounted a horse again, although
the feeling of height and weight and power
stayed with me. Cowboy ways are not the poet's
ways. We lift words off the page, only to settle
them back in place, meaning what they will,

never reined in to turn figure-eights
against a darkening sky, never held fast
to follow a mapped-out route, never led
to water they would not wish to drink,
never silent in the wake of purple storms.

The Great Nemesis

This is the house of death.
I touch the threshold
and spiral downward
into a vortex of adulthood,
youth, childhood, birth,
the womb, the zygote, the ovum,
the sperm, the miraculous
union, the flame of love, the dark,
impenetrable matter of before.

Death shreds my sinews,
crushes my bones. Dust,
ash and smoke flavor my flesh
until it is palatable to the ancients,
to the modern madding crowd.
Centripetal night barrels
down the tunnel of light,
tossing to and fro, crossing,
then retreating from the anarchy

Of desire. Death is the great
nemesis, the awful annihilator
of the *élan vital* and the will
to power. It thrusts and spreads
beyond my loins, up to my brain,
spilling over into the field
of Being in which we move, live,
and flourish, like a grain of corn
buried in the soil.

Flat loaves of bread crawl
across the stony ground,
inching toward the terracotta ovens
that await them. Here poems lie
fallow and faithful, patient

for emergence, trusting
in a shower of ink to scribble forms
on the naked page. Here we thrive
with elemental desire. Here we

eat pieces of dark matter.
O here we die, falling forward
into the house of death,
its crooked door ajar.

Cumbria

(After W. S. Merwin)

Mist devours the hills
in the middle distance
red alders sway
like stalks of wheat
the breathless morning
moves toward the sun
I cannot tell where
the clouds begin
and the sky ends
where I begin
and the lakes end
I ramble through
a world apart

The clay darkens
in the rain
limestone crumbles
into dust
white swirls of smoke
climb heavenward
I have yet to learn how
the evening fades
how my life gives way
to pressure points
my room was spring
yellow and clean
the ground so moist
footsteps carved deep
imprints in the grass
that filled with dew
each dawn

Between the rocks
I swept cobwebs
from the world
the brook bathed
a bed of small stones
holding them in the sun
calling me to blue air
as light poured
through me
alders rose
into the sky
the emptiness
around them
I see sheep
marked red and green
in the meadow
I had forgotten
everything
in the mist
and then
they were there

*Cumbria is a region in northwest England famous for its
stunning lakes and beautiful countryside full of hills—or fells—
that offer popular walking routes. William Wordsworth and
Samuel Taylor Coleridge lived in Grasmere, one of Cumbria's
charming villages.*

Why I Must Fly

An owl calls and I turn my head
as branches of an old cottonwood
creak and moan threatening rupture
and collapse onto the riverbank
where I have come to dig for the family jewels
buried long before my birth buried wholly
in the rocky soil that turns ankles and minds
toward the smooth hills of Paradise cattle graze
as gravity-bound angels feeding on manna and nectar
a diet of steadily chewed grain or let us say cud
but even demeaned the delicacy builds bodies
something angels need not bother with something
we cannot conquer or subdue this side of the grave

An owl calls and I stir the embers of my paltry fire
it threatens to singe the fringe of my Plains jacket
presented to me by the buffalo shaman who foretold
the end of migrant life the end of all life for the keepers
of this land I drop my head in shame but wonder
which piece of the prairie I may preserve and own
first for my pleasure then for the joy of generations
        to come
every life is bound to the promise of unity with the All
the first and last the alpha and omega the cycle
of beginning and end of restarting and hope the current
of the years carrying us away into the netherworld
        of the unknown

An owl calls and I marvel as its long lithe wings
flap toward me aimed directly at my head the target
of this hunter of humanity this oligarch of the darkening
skies guided by eyesight not bound by gravity or doubt
but suited perfectly to the hunt and its tireless pursuit
of prey unwary unwitting innocents ready to be swooped
into the strata of fog that settles on the flat farmland I work

and work into a facsimile of an organic mill of vegetables
and fruits nourishment for body and soul if it needs
to eat to survive which it does not and the owl knows
how one flies with the other how the moon turns the screws
of anxiety and fear into desire for fleshy delights only perfect
flight can reassure the living only dead-on eyes can see
        what's next
wide enough to weigh the world sharp enough to dissect tall
grasses hopeful enough to show me I must fly for prey or die

The Halo of Beauty

Sheep scamper up the fell
as I trudge behind, steadying
my footing grasping stones
aiming for an upright shadow
for my righteous claim to the beauty
that beams as Cumbria's halo
land of mystic showings

I take my place on the ridge whirling
in circles drinking in the view
of prophetic poets questing
for the sublime for ecstasy and joy
this land inspires like an errant muse
seeking whom she may devour in madness
Plato condemned the poet for making
only copies of copies of the really real
we gnaw on them for strength for life
but taste only sand

Here the quest reclaims itself
as the hidden reward
I reach for what I cannot embrace
I thirst for fountains of clear waters
trickling down the fells into open eyes
cleansing the doors of perception
unveiling a graven message
This is not your own

Return of the Country Flaneur

(After V. S. Naipaul)

This is the beginning of things
the idea of emptiness
life forces pushing past the void
incarnate in kaleidoscopes
of creatures precursors
to the cargo of Noah
emissaries of the eternal Yes
combatants with the infernal No
moving gracefully beyond them
wrapped in mist
I cross the infinite dales
gathering glyphs of a summer dawn
like fossils encrusted in tawny fells
like sheep grazing yellow-green pastures
curving lazily past Yorkshire villages

What gifts do I bring to this beginning
how many leagues have I traversed for such a view
enduring my own folly and strangeness
the quarrelsome gait of a country *flaneur*
a shaded lane leads off a road I do not know
the new way there soon gives out
only shadows spill from whitewashed fences
only golden stone houses tout perfectly thatched roofs
the terrain turns rugged
birch trees guard the upward slopes
I reach a break from the woods
see infinity in the middle distance
dull reflections in the mirrored distance
the ordinary emptiness of an ordinary dawn
how many leagues have I traversed to know it

Frisson

The mournful northern winds
howl around the poet's head
a frisson of sorrow and loss
dipped into cold waters of winter
he yearns for Eros' return
warmth tenderness attachment
all missing from his forest hut
fitted solely to his solitary self
a creative garret a hermit's cave
the word alone embraces him
with its two-dimensional weight
black marks on a white page
cold and barren awaiting
the glow of embers
red smoke rising
to the blackened sky
winter's toll on his pilgrim soul
on the vagabond singer
of troubadour refrains
love's labors lost on the winds

I have tracked a bobcat
across my father's field
my steps uncertain
the big cat scooting
into the open his quest uncharted
his port unknown on this sea
of grains and stalks of hay
his lithe movements a study
in fluidity sleek swerves
and pivots across the grasses
now lost to sight now found far
from where I gaze a drifter's trail
a samba into encroaching
shadows of dusk he is free of me

and I of him *Only connect*
the wind chills at the back of my neck
light retires for the night
the troubadour serenades
the poet and bobcat
with timeless songs of Eros
tactile and warm
meant only for he who has ears to hear

White on White

The sense of belonging recedes
into shadows on the hills
they turn brown then white
prematurely aging in a descent
through epochs of unknowing
I have grasped the mother root
of oaks it bores under the soil
buckling the farmhouse floor
white flagstones rise
like a dais in an amphitheater
from the far seats I spy the masked actors
twirling past one another's arms
they stride alone into the tragic chorus
in step with the white of the void whose roar
fades like distant bells in the valley

I have seen cracks in the white earth
fields white for harvest
roads white with dusty clumps of sand
grapes white on the vine
rows upon rows of whitewashed fences
holding back nothing but sky
the day owes little to white foxes in their den
little to flocks of dirty white sheep
or meadows white with flora so wild
in their whiteness yet fringed in blue

I scrape their white paint into my palms
and smear it over my face
I vow a white on white a purity of will
I cultivate a purity of white not found
on the color wheel or in laymen's prisms
light fades to white before the fall of clouds
before the garments of the firmament
put the green world to bed

white dreams will swirl before its eyes
they will tap into the parent root of promise
blooming like lilacs in the white cool of dawn

The Bones of Time

I stalk the creek bank
in search of signs of life
a boot print a hand print
the reflection of his eyes
in the clear trickles baptizing
the smooth flat stones of time

days nights months years
slide into the past gathering husks
of lives they have devoured
where the lives go I do not know
where the waters take us
I cannot say but the mossy banks

absorb my footfalls as dough
receives the baker's imprint
the mark of good measure
the seal of rich grain reserved
only for the finest loaves
we will eat them in the last days

when they come I will be looking
for my father's eyes even closed
they will draw me toward his hut
even blind they will lay me prone
on the creek bed to await the waters
washing over the long flat bones of time

Western

The world spills its dazzling designs
past the lip of the arroyo into the empty
earthen jars of my waiting my anticipating
a rain that will pepper the dust
of my trail to here
I have packed canteens of water
parcels of food into the saddlebag
I hoist over my shoulder
the horse long dead from the heat
monotony and hopelessness
of the trudge through the desert
nothing left to break its fall

I have come to your town to remember
the sun on your face the freckles across
your brow the crooked bump of your nose
your cheek lying on mine in sweet repose
the Earth Woman married us under
the rocky outcrop you blushed a deep innocence
I turned my face to the sky and laughed
like a man released from the gallows
you were my new life that I soon forgot to live

Few other places attract me now
the firmament tightens the miles stretch
to infinity a rough road always ahead
I must walk it until the sun sets
and the night embraces your memory
then I will dream of riding again
of your tender design
as we lay together cheek to cheek

Homecoming

The prairie is alive tonight
all creatures on the odyssey home
carrying the blue jewels of the day
on their heads and backs
the end of evening has been
a long time coming now shadows
stretch their paper-thin bodies
into the blackening sky
I would join them but I am still
without a place to go
this land births little comfort
for the vagabond seeking shelter
from the moon claiming solace
in the nervous winds twisting
through the clover and over hills
frisking me like an arrogant agent
of the TSA my flight requires
no baggage my seat is on the wing
hold on for a bumpy ride
nothing to eat or drink until we land
in the Aegean Sea

My hands are rough and dirty scarred
by hard work eons of scraping by
building shelters for others happy
to move into their new abodes
cut off from their neighbors and friends
an elaborate hermitage of the soul
but who speaks of it today who looks
into it searching its depth its breadth
its breaths of exhilaration and gloom
the prairie is on fire

I knew a man like me out of prison
after so many years no skills to sell

nothing to buy cut loose in the breeze
of an autumn morning free to travel
in any direction free to move and leap
into the traffic flow until the cars stopped
and he laughed into the sun at their honking
like geese he had forgotten them making their way
south to a permanent breeding ground
of backbreaking work and great loss
he died I heard from a bullet in the brain
a robbery gone wrong guns firing at masks
a bloody smile stuck to his face

Initiated into the Eleusinian mysteries each creature
practices the ritual of nothingness writ large
across the empty sky like lodestars
their thoughts guide me toward my place in the prairie
the observer changing what he observes
the looter snatching food and drink from the source
nature nurtures we are told but the rotting trees
the red tooth and claw feed me with only fear
of mortality the angst of finitude the promise
of plenitude in currents of the prairie carrying
weary sailors home into Ithaca's harbor
the jewels of a lifetime in hand

Canyon

The glassy rocks
bear our weight
in the distance
low voices
of the ancestors
we hear only
the river rush
to unseen depths
we know only
what we cannot know

Sure footing slips away
into the canyon
it is not my time to fall
I peer into the sky
waiting for
the change to come
something is about
to happen
but I must make
its meaning

Scrapes of petroglyphs
climb nowhere
the breath of dawn
bittersweet breeze
this is not the path
of triumph this is not
the path of peace

* * *

The ancient stone fence
crumbles and sways
it holds back nothing

berries and birds
grow where they will
the rock face trembles
the Earth moves
something is about
to happen

Prodigal Words

We knew there were better words
to use before the parting
circuitous arcane words
words disconnected
from the shielded glances
we cast back
at the wounds
in the woods
bear traps
lay open to rust
dead stalks of willow
crowded the pond
it glistened in the breeze
white ridges over brackish green

When the deer came
we drank mulled wine
and celebrated the return
of living flesh
of life not resigned
to winter's
bleak box of death
then we needed
prodigal words
words of betrayal and return
words of forgiveness and regret

Now with the windows
shut against the cold
no words can enter
none know why
they must die so young
in the breath
that birthed them

POSTLUDE

"I will do water—beautiful, blue water."
–Claude Monet

Yes

1.

Your body says *Yes*
to the clean,
well-lighted night,
an embrace of the wild.

You rise aflutter,
a spiral of pale blue
ribbons encircles
your hair, your waist,
your arms, your legs.

Above the red-black
earth, you wander
in exile, expelled
from your homeland,
cast into the incipient
perils of the blue, blue self.

2.

Rain peppers the ceramic
tiles of orange, green
and maroon like champagne
spilling from an emerald
magnum, bubbles pooling
in U-shaped cradles along
the rugged roof line.

Splatters smear
the ink on your papers,
leaving wells of black,
as magic words drain
across the page.

Too much water kills,
too many poems fill
the scrolls of ancient
sages meditating on
the mystery of the world:
why it exists instead
of the fire and flux that
leave nothing saturated
or sustained, nothing solid
or pure, only the flame-fed
kindling of night.

3.

I say *Yes* to your body
as it floats overhead,
aimlessly advancing,
restlessly recovering
the iridescent glow
of stars, polished
with the brilliance
of novenas and novas,
of the nervous pacing
of God.

Beyond the reaches
of time, the future
homesteads the past,
laying down roots
of memory tangled
in threads of desire.
Footholds in the sheer
sides of buttes, lathered
in orange, deposits
of desert winds,

and the softest
clay. You sculpt
your figure into the cliff,
cover it in diaphanous
designs of grazing deer,
yearning for clarity,
meaning and rest.
The body knows only water
and blood, splashing
them on the red and black earth,
burbling in rivulets of *Yes*.

This Time

(After James Wright)

The cold winter moon
spills its luminous
jewels of fire
past the edge
of the road.

The night wind shudders
at the sound.
I turn my head.

In the distance,
wings light upon branches.

The long sad bones
of my hands cut deep
into blue stones.

This time, I have left
something behind me.

In open grasses
I will dream of placid water.

About the Author

Arlice W. Davenport is the author of three collections of poems, *Setting the Waves on Fire, Everlasting: Poems,* and *Kind of Blue: New Poems,* published respectively by Meadowlark Press (2020) and Meadowlark Poetry Press (2021 & 2022). He is the retired Books editor and Travel editor for *The Wichita Eagle* newspaper. He and his wife, Laura, continue their travels, which include more than 30 stays in Europe. Below is his self-portrait in verse. Enjoy.

Icarus and Orpheus

At last I see the future coming my way
the arrival of an enigma the solidity
of a Greek sponge dived for
near Tarpon Springs fishing nets
surround me on the Florida coast
they cast across my shoulders
a gaping albatross around my neck
how serendipitous that I am reading
Coleridge the visionary poet the seer
the professor attuned to the dark ground
of Being the unseen foundation of all that is

I am a poet and a pilgrim pulled by every
magnetic field on the compass face
trekking the world then re-presenting it in poems
what I seek is not the Holy Grail
nor a relic of the early saints I am after
the abiding source of beauty in the world

it transcends us it befriends us kin to the soul
manifesting as the good the true the really real
my poems dive into these depths not for glory
or vanity but to hold fast the reality that embraces me
beauty is its sublime vehicle I watch it move
and marvel at its timeless perfection of form

I have fashioned a psyche from the rigors
of travel and am always the Other whether
in Europe China New Zealand Mexico the Philippines
and beyond each site pins down a piece of my self
each shapes the direction of my life as a *telos*
as a goal to be pursued outside the doors of great mysteries
they reside in the ancient tales of the mystics
who saw Aphrodite uniting couples
in love who supplicated the gods
and spirits wherever the sacred reigned

How can my poems capture this re-create it
how can my poems create themselves
few answers come to me at this stage of life
few options preserve my sense of will
free of all tyranny to determine my habits of being
my wingspan to fly above the fray then collapse
too near the sun I am Icarus and Orpheus
sailing above the sea to a melody of siren songs
they say home is but a mirage the voyage forward
shimmers as the only place of belonging
may I still have eyes turned inward when I reach it

Acknowledgments

As the head of Meadowlark Books, publisher **Tracy Million Simmons** runs a tight ship. Her warm and all-knowing leadership has kept me on deck through three books now. My debt to her is enormous; without her I would still be filing my poems in a manilla folder, hidden from the world's view. Now, thanks to her confidence in me, we have published again. I offer her endless thanks for that.

Linzi Garcia has beautifully grown into her role as my book designer and editor. We share a love of philosophy along with poetry. Her attention to detail, speed, efficiency and incorrigible optimism let me know that my poems are in good hands to see the light of day. She has done double duty this time around, also editing and designing my chapbook, *O How the Sea Mourns*. She deserves a hearty round of applause.

My great friend **Norman Carr** has perfected his latest calling as an abstract painter, and he has graced the cover of this book with another of his beautiful works. His talent, prolific output, intelligent sensibility and humble demeanor all make him an artistic saint. He has blessed me in uncounted ways. Long may he paint.

And a word of gratitude to **Roy Beckemeyer**, whom I like to call the Godfather of Kansas Poets. His vigorous leadership, boundless depth of poetic knowledge and always inspiring verse have spurred me on since I first met him at a meeting of the Kansas Authors Club. He is a poetic and personal treasure, not least for his masterful appreciation of this book, which alone is worth the price of admission. I owe him much, as well.

Finally, my beautiful wife, **Laura**, has patiently endured my many hours on a laptop searching for *le mot juste*. This, of course, requires constant editing. That she indulges me in this creative enterprise makes her, too, a modern-day saint. All my love to her.

Meadowlark POETRY

Books are a way to explore, connect, and discover. Poetry incites us to observe and think in new ways, bridging our understanding of the world with our artistic need to interact with, shape, and share it with others.

Publishing poetry is our way of saying—

We love these words,
we want to preserve them,
we want to play a role in sharing them
with the world.

Meadowlark Press
— since 2014 —

meadowlarkpoetrypress.com

This is poetry of intellectual breadth built on a foundation of honest emotional depth. I encourage you to take up this book and read, to follow Davenport's best advice: "Your heart is bruised, bleeding / drops of unrequited love. / The viscera of your body / tighten like a noose. You could slide // your head into it, if you choose, / . . . Love flees / like a deer bounding in a forest. / You are too broken to give chase . . . / . . . Let poems be your new heart. // It will not bleed."
— Roy J. Beckemeyer, Kansas Authors Club Poet of the Year, *Mouth Brimming Over*

Everlasting is Arlice W. Davenport's second poetry collection—inspired by religion, mythology, philosophy, travel, and classic art. The diction, style, and subject matter differ in each of the four sections of the book: "Into the Mystic," "Finding a Self," "Patterns of Fecundity," and "Other Shores." The diction ranges from plainstyle to lofty, the style from traditional to free verse, and subjects span the breadth of internal, earthly, and mystical experiences, observations, and questions. Each poem, ranging from one to two pages in length, deserves focus, as Davenport pays close attention to every detail in every poem and the effect each poem has on the entire collection—tokens of his careful craftsmanship. Overall, this book depicts life as a piece of art—beautiful and meant to be savored.

Made in the USA
Columbia, SC
24 July 2022

63798204R00067